FORWARD

"Death and Life lie in the power of the tongue".
The Word of God is clear in describing the primary purpose of the tongue, which is to be used as a creative force. Unfortunately, many do not understand this principle and therefore use words loosely without any thought of the kind of power they are unleashing. Learn how to use the inherent power of speech to deliver destiny into your hands"

- Dr Abiodun Oyebola

TONGUE TIED

Proverbs 18:11

"Death and Life lie in the power of the tongue"......

The tongue is a muscular organ located inside the mouth. It has several functions including helping with chewing and moving food around the oral cavity. It aids in initiating swallowing and most important of all plays a role in speech and language development.

In pediatrics, we often see children who are born with a

correctable anomaly of the tongue known as a *"tongue-tie"* or *ankylogossia*.

In this condition, the tongue is attached to the floor of the oral cavity by a band of tissue and depending on severity, could lead to initial difficulties with feeding and swallowing in the newborn. So literally the tongue can't function properly.

If left un-corrected, it may affect the child's ability to speak clearly and fluently, particularly with pronunciations. The treatment is to take out the band of tissue that *ties down* the tongue, thereby releasing the tongue. This procedure is called the Tongue-release.

Let's look at this verse again. **Proverbs 18:11** *"Death and Life lie in the **POWER OF THE TONGUE**....*

There is power in the tongue. There are many Christians who are tongue-tied. They are not using the tongue God has given them because they are not aware of its spiritual function. They are spiritually tongue-tied. Let me submit to you that the tongue has power. Tremendous power.

That muscular organ in your mouth is loaded with unlimited power. That power is stronger than the fiercest tsunami or biggest hurricane ever recorded. James, the Apostle, describes the tongue (even though a small member of the human body) as a rudder (steering) that controls a ship.

God's word, the Bible says, "DEATH and LIFE lie in the power of the tongue." Because the Word says so, that settles it. The power in your tongue can produce life or death. Profound!

The tongue is the ORGAN OF SPEAKING. So, the power

lies in the SPEAKING (indirectly through your tongue.)

Jesus speaking to his disciples in **John 6:63** "*The words that I SPEAK to you, they are spirit and they are life*".

Are you tongue tied? Unable to speak as you should? Or are you speaking life or death?

GOD'S IMAGE

What you say can be CREATIVE (Life) or DESTRUCTIVE (Death).

You may not believe it, but God says so. Your words have power in them. In the book of Genesis chapter one, God literally spoke the world into existence! *He created everything we see and feel by WORDS*; and we were created in the image of God, so what God does we can do.

Listen, even though the words were initially thoughts in

the mind of God, He had to give VOICE to His thoughts.

The mind is where our thoughts are born. It is not enough to think positive thoughts. It is not enough to think the right thoughts. These are important and is the starting point, but the power lies in saying the right words.

God spoke (voiced out His thoughts) and created the universe, including man. We are created in His image.

Genesis 1:26 "And God said, let us create man in our own *image* and after our *likeness*.

I was speaking to our church group and I was explaining what the image of an object is. An image is a replica (sort of). It is not a substitute but rather it is the object reflecting itself.

So, using a mirror, whatever the original does (the object), the image does also.

When you stand in front of a mirror, you see yourself in the mirror. Obviously, that's your image. Whatever you do or can do, your image also does in the mirror.

That is why the term "mirror image" is used. Therefore, if we are created in the image of God, we are mirror images of God. It means we can do what God does. We have God-like capacities within us. ***This means if God can create with words, so can you and me.*** Until you understand this concept, you can't live a completely victorious life.

WORDS HAVE INHERENT POWER

My journey is littered with so many testimonies of how God has fulfilled His promises in my life.

There are times when the Lord will drop "something" in my spirit and no matter how impossible it may seem, once I begin to say what the Lord says, it is usually only a matter of time before I begin to see its manifestation.

John 6:63 "The words that I speak to you, they are spirit and they are life"

The word spirit there starts with a small **s**. It is not capital S as in the Holy Spirit.

Psalm 127:3-5 says "Behold, Children are a HERITAGE from the LORD, the fruit of the womb is a reward".

Heritage means i*nheritance*, to *inherit*. I will never forget that night in our one-bedroom apartment on the Westside of Chicago. We asked the Lord for our heritage, our inheritance.

We put pen on paper, asking the Lord to bless us with a boy. But we didn't stop there. We told the Lord the qualities and the attributes we wanted in our son. My wife and I were specific as much as possible. The Lord told us to give our unborn child a name; we chose Caleb.

Before Caleb became a life form in his mother's womb, he had a name. We spoke about him. ***We aligned ourselves with the maker and began to create realities from our desires.*** We did the same before our daughter was born.

Whatever is lifeless in your life, whatever situation has remained dormant or impossible, maybe the Lord is asking you today to speak to it.

Your words have the power to transform what's lifeless into a living soul.

YOUR LIFE REFLECTS YOUR WORDS

Proverbs 6:2. *"You have been **trapped by what you say**, ensnared by the words of your mouth....* (NIV).

*"you have **trapped yourself** by your agreement and are caught by what you said"* .... (NLT).

Your life reflects your words. God can't be blamed or mocked here. He has handed that power over to you to determine what you allow and disallow in your life.

You must watch what you say! Some folks are battling sickness, financial woes, setbacks because they have trapped themselves literarily .... with their words.

"*You have trapped yourself by your agreement*" .... That is profound! Our words can dig holes that we then fall into. **When you speak, you are making an agreement.**

I personally believe what the Bible means here is that whatever you say, God stamps "approved" on it! Regardless of what it is. So really, you are in the driver's seat.

For example, if I ask you a rhetorical question, "Do you have $20,000 in your account as down payment for your new home purchase?"

If you don't have that amount available to you, you can answer that question several ways, but how you answer is key!

You can say "No, I don't have the $20,000 right now, but God will supply and provide all my needs" ....OR

"No, I don't have $20,000, I am broke, OR

"No, I will never have that kind of money".

But thank God, the same tongue that can get you into trouble can also get you out of trouble. The same tongue that can build self-made prisons is also used as a jail break.

Which is the better response? If you say you are broke, you have just empowered the spirit of lack/poverty in your life. Remember "the words I speak are spirit and life (breath of life). Do not give life to poverty or negativity or impossibility by your words (tongue).

Also saying "No, I will never have that kind of money"; that response is equally wrong. You have legally set a limitation on your life that will prove to be an unscalable wall. A trap and a snare. Don't do it! Again, **Proverbs 6:2** "you have trapped yourself by your agreement".

Sometime in the past, my wife and I decided it was time to buy a home.

Sometime in the past, my wife and I decided it was time to buy a home. After months of searching and praying, we finally settled on a single unit home. At that time, we didn't have the money for a down payment, but I knew the Lord had told me "it is time for us to buy". I told my wife this and we both agreed.

We stepped out in faith standing on God's word and contacted our local bank. From that moment on till we located our destined home, we kept speaking what we wanted to see. We had a detailed list of our desires and most importantly we declared the supernatural supply of the resources we needed.

My wife and I would drive down to this empty house (with the kids in the car) and thank God for our new home. We were fully persuaded like Abraham, that God was able to do the impossible.

The sale was a miracle because the seller wanted a long closing. Six months! The good news was, we also needed those six months to get our down payment ready. What a mighty God we serve! God connected us at the right time to the right seller. Why? Because we aligned our speaking with our believing. We never said no, this is impossible. **If God says something is yours, all He needs you to do is agree with Him.**

Please do not say *"I don't have the money so that's it"*. You should say, *"I may not have the money now, but MY GOD SHALL SUPPLY ALL MY NEEDS ACCORDING TO HIS RICHES IN GLORY THROUGH CHRIST JESUS"*

Begin to engage your tongue today, speak what God says about you. Create possibilities with your words. Build the future you want to see by speaking about it today.

ARM YOURSELF WITH GODS WORD (KNOWLEDGE)

If you say, "I don't have $20,000; I am broke". I'm just being honest. ***You can be honest but also ignorant.*** Ignorance is not an excuse. As a matter of fact, ignorance can be lethal.

"My people perish for lack of knowledge" - **Hosea 2:3**. Ignorance has literally cost so many lives, livelihoods, marriages, and so on.

Satan will always exploit your areas of ignorance. Once

you know what you have in Christ
(divine access), and you know
what belongs to you in Christ (His
promises); then begin to declare
it in *agreement* with God.

UNLEASH THE GOD POTENTIAL IN YOU

Let us go back to **Genesis 1:27-28**, the story of creation. After God created man (in His image), He now reveals why He created him (in His image).

"God blessed them; and God said to them, "Be *fruitful and multiply* and *fill the earth* and *subdue it: and rule over* the fish of the sea and over the birds of the sky and over every living thing that moves on the earth"

This is quite a tall order for God to give man. God expects

the following from His children
based on the above text:

1. Be fruitful: Fruitfulness
2. Multiply: Productivity
3. Fill the earth: Increase
4. Subdue it: Dominion
5. Rule over: Authority

How were Adam and Eve
supposed to be fruitful, be
productive, increase, have
dominion, and rule over all things
God created?

Just like God rules by His
Words. We rule with our words,
our tongue. Isaiah states it quite
simply, **Isaiah 55:10-11** " For as
the rain cometh down and the
snow from heaven and returneth

not hither, but watereth the earth and it bring forth and bud, that it may give seed to the sower and bread to the eater:
So shall MY WORD be that *goeth forth out of my mouth*: it shall not return unto me void, but it shall *accomplish* that which I please, and i*t shall prospe*r in the thing whereto I sent it.

This very descriptive verse makes it clear that just like rain falls and soaks the ground, causing things to grow; so, your words can cause things to grow in your life. You too can release God's inspired words into your life and watch it accomplish and prosper in the thing where *to you sent it.*

Things just don't happen in your life. ***Your words create your environment.*** You can speak life into your situation or entrap yourself by negative words.

Decide today to speak inspired words over your health, your family, your children, over your finances and even into your future. Say what you want to see. You want to live a healthy and long life? declare out loud the word of the Lord- **Psalm 91:16** "with long life I will satisfy you and show you my salvation"

Remember you are meant to be fruitful, to be productive, to increase, to have dominion and rule like Kings.

"Who has made us kings and priests unto God and His father; to him be glory and dominion for ever and ever."- Revelations 1:6

WHAT'S AT STAKE?

Proverbs 18:11

"Death and Life lie in the power of the tongue" ......

Our words dominate us. You will either rise or fall based on your words. Literally, life or death is at your command. The quality of life you enjoy depends on what you say.

Proverbs 13:3 (GNT) says "Be careful what you say and protect your life. A careless talker destroys himself". **The NKJV says,** "He who guards his mouth preserves his life; But he who

pens wide his lips shall have
destruction".

It's not too late to start
speaking the words of life and
faith into your situation. Once you
understand the power of the
tongue, you can begin to create
the world and environment you
desire just by your speaking in
faith.

Load your heart with the truth
of God's word. Engage in
speaking the Word of life;
download into your heart words
of faith and begin to speak out
those words. Say to sickness, "be
healed in Jesus name". To lack,
"my God shall supply all my

needs according to His riches in glory".

<u>HOW TO UNLEASH THE POWER OF THE TONGUE</u>

You can't say what you don't know. Information is key. Knowledge is vital to speaking. That's the whole essence of educating yourself. Begin to spend time in God's word and meditate upon it. Soak up His words in your spirit, let them percolate and become part of your spirit. Once that happens, whatever you say coming from your spirit is empowered to prosper.

If your thinking is not right, then your speaking will not be right. Align your thoughts with Gods word, conform them to His precepts, and then you begin to speak. **Matthew 12:24** "out of the abundance of the heart, the mouth speaks.

The abundance of the heart! Another translation puts it this way "*out of the overflow of the heart.*...

So how can you speak life when there are no life words in your heart?

For your speaking to be effective, you must have an abundance of His words locked up in your heart.

Don't be in a hurry to speak or declare Gods promises until you have meditated upon it, believing it, then you can speak with authority. ***Meditating on God's word releases faith in you. FAITH IS WHAT EMPOWERS GODS WORD***.

When you speak Gods words in faith, you are acting like God Himself. That word will always deliver.

Isaiah 55:11 "So shall my word be THAT GOETH FORTH OUT OF MY MOUTH, it shall not return to me void, but it shall *accomplish* that which I please and it shall prosper in the thing whereto I sent it"

Your words spoken in faith, must accomplish that which it was sent to. Jesus speaking to his disciples reiterated the power of the tongue in **Mark 11:23** "For assuredly, I say to you, whoever SAYS to this mountain, "be removed and be cast into the sea, and does not doubt in his heart, but believes that those things he SAYS will be done, he will have whatsoever he SAYS"

Do you see the number of times the Lord puts emphasis on say? You must say what you have in abundance in your heart.

God is bound by HIS WORD. God's word binds Him in a sense. He can't go against His word. That is why He can never lie. Psalm 138:2 says "I will worship towards Your holy temple and praise Your lovingkindness and Your truth; FOR YOU HAVE MAGNIFIED YOUR WORD ABOVE ALL YOUR NAME.

God has elevated his word above all his names. Did you see that? God has many wonderful names. Yet, the LORD tells us HIS WORD IS HIGHER than all his names combined.

And we have that same capacity as our God has. After all, He made us in His image. Let His words paint the picture on the canvas of your life. Let His words bind you.

Proverbs 6:2 "You are ensnared by the words of your mouth; you are taken by the words of your mouth. Let them ensnare you. It is a wonderful thing for God's word to ensnare us or trap us. It means we will never be able to escape the blessings He has for us once we are trapped by His words. His blessings will catch up to you and overtake you.

LET US PRAY

Lord today, I pray for a spiritual tongue release. I am no longer tongue-tied. I receive the grace to begin to fill my heart with your words. I also receive the grace to begin to believe your word and to speak it into every situation. I will

enjoy the fruits of speaking life
into my world. Amen.

About the Author

Dr Oyebola is a man called and appointed by God in these times with a unique voice to speak to the issues of our day. His message seeks to remove the blindfold that keeps God's people from entering their place of rest.

Dr Oyebola is the Senior Pastor of Nations Light House Church in Mississauga, Ontario Canada. He's also a practicing Pediatrician in Hamilton, Ontario. He's married to Lola Oyebola and they have two children.

www.ingramcontent.com/pod-product-compliance
Lightning Source LLC
Chambersburg PA
CBHW060101050426
42448CB00011B/2568